The
Keys

Unlocking the door to who you are

Mary Ann Dawson, Ph.D.

Edited by Yvonne D. Petrin

iUniverse, Inc.
New York Bloomington

The Keys
Unlocking the Door to Who You Are

Copyright © 2008 by Mary Ann Dawson

iUniverse books may be ordered through booksellers or by contacting:

iUniverse
1663 Liberty Drive
Bloomington, IN 47403
www.iuniverse.com
1-800-Authors (1-800-288-4677)

ISBN: 978-0-595-48365-5 (pbk)
ISBN: 978-0-595-71798-9 (cloth)
ISBN: 978-0-595-60456-2 (ebk)

Printed in the United States of America

Dedication

I dedicate this book to my family: my husband John, daughter Bianca, and son Blake, for without them none of this would be possible.

Acknowledgement

Thank you to my furry children who kept me company while I was writing this book: my Akitas Raphael, Phoenix, Noah, and Geisha; my cats Sapphire, Gianni, Sally, Porsche, Simba, Bentley, Charlie, and Tigger.

Thank you Pat Limosani for all your extra input, you truly made a difference.

Special thanks to my friend and editor, Yvonne Petrin, for without her there is NO WAY this book would have gone to print. The Keys worked for me to attract a writer spirit who helped me realize a dream.

Table of Contents

Foreword

When I was a little girl I gave my parents a hard time about the mysteries of God. Devout Catholics who never questioned dogma, they believed the rules of the Church were the law. I had an instinct, however, that there was more to be known and there was a design to God's universe, and I wanted to know how it all worked. After years of studying religion and metaphysics, I embarked on a personal journey to discover life's spiritual mysteries.

I wish for all who read this to follow their own spiritual journey and to see life's many blessings along the path. Happiness is found along the journey, not at the journey's end.

Introduction

The potential for living a full life is locked inside you, yet you do not know how to open yourself up. Enclosed are simple, life-changing keys to break the chains that bind you to an unfulfilled life and to help you reach your personal and professional goals. Using these keys will unlock your life and open it to joy, happiness, love, wealth, and health, God's greatest gifts to all who wish to accept them.

In this book you will find The Keys to create and recreate who you need to be. Some of The Keys will fit your locked heart, for example, and unlock it with one turn; others may require a few turns to unlock your mind or spirit. Maybe you are unhealthy from disease or from toxic relationships with your spouse, family, friends, peers, or coworkers. The Keys will unlock barriers to the love, health, and wealth that you desire and deserve; you can stop illness, make money, bring love into your life, or find fulfillment. You do not have to sell your soul for these great blessings, but as you grow spiritually these blessings will remain with you.

The Universe is abundant and is meant for your experience and enjoyment. True abundance on all levels comes from developing a prosperous "consciousness" which is the result of ideas held in your mind. Your mind is an incredible thinking machine which can create and recreate anything in your life. Examples of this are a new job, a mate to share life with, improved health, or financial success. All of this is at your fingertips when you put The Keys in place.

The Keys will unlock the doors to your mind, heart and spirit to reveal the path for your personal divine purpose. Although you cannot unfasten the doors for others, when you apply The Keys to yourself, negativity will be released, and your positive energy will affect your friends, family and anyone with whom you come in contact. Believing God is benign in nature and seeking to live by the universal laws allows The Keys to unlock your "doors" and will lead you on a "lighted" path.

Apply The Keys and you will receive blessings on every level of your existence. If you open your mind to The Keys, you will achieve wholeness.

I invite you to take The Keys and hold them in your mind, unlocking the door to a whole new world. May this book light your path as you learn a new way of thinking to produce abundance and goodness every day of your life.

Chapter 1:
The God-Human Connection

I. The One Source

Everything you see on earth is made from the One Source, God. It does not matter what name you choose: Universal Being, The All-knowing, Love, God, Goddess, Buddha, Allah, The Omnipresent, or Supreme Being. All that matters is what you believe and what you are comfortable with.

You are made of God, The Original Substance, and God wants you to live your life with all that is possible. God wants you to experience the most abundant and satisfying life, because God lives and enjoys creations though humanity, working within each one of us through our thoughts, words, and actions.

You are a soul embodied in flesh, and you are flesh imbued with a soul: a spark of Divinity. A soul having a human experience, not a human having a soul experience, you are an expression of the Creator; you are part of all that is. This is true even if you are not aware of it. Search to find yourself. Like a newborn baby, be open to learning about life and the world around you without limitations or fears.

You are the highest form of biological organism containing consciousness. A higher state of awareness which taps into the Divine Power hidden inside of you, consciousness is the voice within and it is directed by your mind. Just as all energy is a manifestation of God's will, the underdeveloped power in your consciousness is an expression of God's will. Because you were created in God's image and likeness, you possess His power, His intelligence, and, most importantly, His love. Therefore, your consciousness is God's consciousness as well as the consciousness of every living thing, and you possess the innate ability to give birth to infinite treasures of creation.

For centuries religion has portrayed a punishing, vengeful God waiting to throw evildoers into hell for breaking His laws. However, God is loving, and God is on your side. God is present in every moment of your life, and prayer empowers your connection to God. You do not need to do anything special to qualify for God's intervention. We have all asked ourselves these questions before as we sought prayer in the face of life's crises. Life is a mystery, and we all need a flame to light our way through the dark times while we struggle to reveal our connection with the Divine.

It is natural to have a desire for increased wealth and health, a successful career and loving relationships. It is not greedy or selfish it is simply the desire for a more abundant life. God desires for you to have everything you want to have and wants you to make the most of your life in the physical body. God does not require you to sacrifice yourself for others; yet when you make the most of yourself you help others, because your peaceful demeanor affects people in a positive way.

Every one of us has at one time felt an energy we didn't know how to explain. We felt a touch on the arm then turned to look and no one was there. We sensed a caring presence breathing around us, but nobody was there. We smelled the aroma of fresh flowers, yet none were in the room. This is how God makes you aware of His Presence. God's Energy is all around you, and these phenomena are evidence of God's Love for you. When you learn how to tap into God's Energy through prayer, your life will change for the better.

God lives and breathes though humanity; through us He desires expression. God uses our hands to build beautiful things, to play beautiful music, to paint landscapes. God runs with our feet, views the world's beauty through our eyes, speaks truths and sings songs with our voices. God intends for humanity to have health and happiness. He wants those who can play music to have instruments and the means to spread their talents. God wants those who appreciate beauty to be able to surround themselves with it. And this goes on and on! God wants all of these things because it is He who enjoys and appreciates them; it is God who wants to play, sing, dance, enjoy beauty, proclaim the truth. It is God who works in you to will and to act.

God, the One Source, is a loving being interested in nothing but your happiness. If that means you need your health restored or money in your wallet, God wants that for you. Due to your upbringing and other factors in your life, however, you might feel God is unreachable and you are unworthy, or you might feel guilty about asking and receiving good things in your life. Yet, you have the right to be happy! You cannot truly be happy or satisfied, however, if your mind and spirit are not living fully in every function. Life is the complete expression of what you can give through your body, mind, and spirit, and there are consequences for denying any one of these three aspects of self. When you fail to live fully engaged with your body, mind, or spirit, you deny God's experience of your soul's expression.

II. Body, Mind, Spirit

You are a spirit interconnected with all other spirits and with the spirit of God. Prayer and faith are simply bridges to God's energy that already resides inside of you. God is your earth, your foundation, your walls, and your roof. Because God is Spirit, He is always with you and within you; God lives in your heart. You are not separate from God, but you are unable to observe this because of the limitations of physical reality. And because you are distracted by the hustle, bustle, and busyness of life, you do not see your connection with God. Remember: the Source is in you and you are part of the Source, and the ultimate purpose of life is to find the nature of God within you.

Your spirit is an imperishable part of God that is in a phase of expression called Nature. Nature is friendly to your life plans; everything you need is naturally there for you. Nature is a renewing force that keeps you in balance. Accept in your mind this is true, because the nature of your life is determined by your inner attitudes. It is essential that your inner purpose harmonize with Nature.

Your body is a physical expression of mind and spirit. Spirit is the God part within you, and your mind enables you to use your spirit. You cannot live fully in your body without food, clothing, and shelter or a place to rest. You cannot live fully in the mind if you like to read and study about things and never have the time or opportunity to do so. To be able to live fully in the spirit you must have love, and you must be able to give and receive love.

In not giving and receiving love, illness and other physical ailments develop because you deplete yourself of the love that is inside of you. Your spirit needs this love to maintain physical health. When you fail to live in love, you are consistently made aware of even the smallest negative things around you, and this ultimately produces effects on the inside that cause illness and disease, whether mental or physical.

For instance, let's say you have a job that you constantly complain about: I hate my job; I am not appreciated; I do not make enough money. These persistent, negative thoughts attract negative energy to you, intensifying the strength of the negativity in your workplace. With not one bit of love for yourself or anything around you, you act as a drain on any positive energy, and you prevent yourself from living in harmony with yourself and your co-workers. What you complain about becomes your reality: you are blamed for your co-worker's incompetence, you don't get a raise, and you hate your job even more.

You have become accustomed to the drama in your life. If you were to let go of all the negativity you would be letting go of the drama that justifies the way you have been acting for years. Unfortunately, nothing does more damage to the body, mind, and spirit than unresolved anger and negativity.

The "law of experiences" dictates that you become what happens to you. Your everyday experiences, health, family relationships, and job skills are a barometer which indicates if you are growing and functioning in harmony with your body, mind, and spirit. Because for many years you have endured a narrow existence, you have unknowingly blocked your life force from getting through to your whole being. If you are living a spiritually impoverished life in this abundant universe, you are not fully conscious. If you are living a narrow existence, you are not expressing your true self; you are cheating yourself. Yet, you possess the power to change all of this!

You can unlock yourself to become receptive. Stop telling other people what you want. Telling others what you desire detours you from getting what you want, because other people cannot give that to you; only God can. Open yourself to God; tell it all to the One Source of All Good. If you are feeling troubled, stop thinking about what is troubling you and think about God instead. Focusing on God instead of on your problems, your problems will disappear, because God attracts the appropriate people and circumstances to help you fully experience life, and He provides amazing channels of abundance for you. Remember, there is no limit to God's power.

Love is a magnet that will attract the very best for you in every situation. Before you go to bed at night and upon waking in the morning, hold fixed in your mind thoughts of love for yourself and for the whole world. Doing this allows your body, mind and spirit to merge. By loving with all of your spirit, the lock will be unfastened from your heart, and you will prosper as you begin to use all of your innate powers. If you start to have the attitude that life is not for getting, but for giving, the God part inside of you will unlock the closed doors placed before you.

There are many paths to God's light and love. To understand the true nature of your spirit is to understand that God is the part of your spirit, infused with love and light. God's love is infused in each and every one of us. By being able to love yourself you will love God and all others around you.

When your intention is love for yourself and others, your spirit will lead you to fulfillment. Working with your spirit and trusting what is inside you provides opportunities for God's Light to manifest through you in the physical realm. This allows you to promote love, tolerance, inclusiveness, and compassion.

Many of you are asked to accept a concept of God and your own spirit which does not allow you to ask questions. You were taught that asking questions was doubting the fixed "word of God." Maybe you were taught that everything is God's will and God will fix everything, relinquishing your own responsibility for any of the decisions you make in your life. So, when things do not turn out the way you expect them to or life becomes challenging, you give up and turn away from God because you feel you are being unfairly punished, and you wonder why God is allowing bad things to happen to you.

In order for you to build a strong spiritual foundation you must explore your faith with understanding and awareness. Developing a strong foundation will allow you to go through life's challenges and to grow. Having a strong foundation will also help you be a source of strength for others.

This world has been blessed with many teachers of spiritual truth who have taught us much about love and responsibility. Gaining spiritual knowledge and understanding is a life process. To be able to gain spiritual knowledge, you must listen with both your physical ears and you inner ears: your intuition. God speaks to us in so many different ways; you need to be patient and learn to be still and listen.

As you allow the One Power that flows though everything and dwells in all things to manifest in your life, you will be empowered to live your life more fully. The Keys will unlock every mystery that has been hidden from you; they will unlock the doors to heaven and earth's wisdom and power, allowing you to be one with The Source.

Chapter 2:
Inside Out

Key 1: Release Toxic Emotions

- *F.E.A.R. = False Evidence Appearing Real*
- *Symptoms of F.E.A.R. = Anger and Worry*
- *What's on the inside manifest on the outside*
- *Toxic emotions make you sick*
- *Toxic emotions blacken your world.*

I. The Problem with Worry, Fear, Anger, & Negativity

You are responsible for everything that happens to you, and your outer success is a result of your inner attitudes. Therefore, there is a direct relationship between your mental and emotional attitudes and the condition of your body as well as what happens in your world. Obsessing over worry and fear leads you away from obtaining what you desire, and you cannot be relieved of unhealthy conditions until you change your thinking. Getting rid of negative attitudes allows positive ones to surface, when you focus your attention on the positive, you eliminate the negative. Once you have removed negative thoughts and actions from your life, goodness, balance, and harmony are restored.

If you want to change the world, the first place to start is within yourself. Once you learn to no longer be afraid of what is inside you, you will no longer be afraid of what is in the world. Once you love and accept yourself, you will be more tolerant and fair-minded to live and let live, to honor and respect others. And with your individual changes you will affect the environment around you.

You have heard of the "law of attraction": like attracts like. Because your thoughts produce what you imagine, you attract and produce things in your life by communicating what you desire in your thoughts. Your attitudes and behaviors are a direct result of what you think. Whatever you identify with in your thoughts, words, and actions, you invite into your life. Whatever you talk about, you draw into your life. Whatever you notice, you lure into your life. Therefore, if you notice or talk about and identify with war, crime, disease, financial scarcity, or disharmony, you will experience these things.

Always remember the "law of attraction" when working with The Keys: If you surround yourself with positive energy, you invite harmony into your life; if you surround yourself with negativity, you attract discord into your life.

Because they block your perception, worry and fear lead you away from personal and spiritual growth. Fear, or **F**alse **E**vidence **A**ppearing **R**eal, is a stressor that causes you to be unhealthy or to act in a counterproductive way, and anger and worry are symptoms of fear. To keep your mind free from anger, worry, and fear, focus on a higher power than yourself.

Negative feelings are not true feelings; rather they are pre-programmed thoughts about something based on a previous experience. Perhaps as a child you were shamed by your Parents and repeatedly told you were "no good" and "stupid." As an adult, nothing you do is good enough; you always feel incompetent and, even though you have a college degree and successful career, you can't quell that nagging voice in your subconscious chiding, "You dummy!" However, you can retrain your mind to think differently about new experiences, and when you do this, your spirit follows and builds a new interpretation of your reality. Whenever that voice hisses at you say to yourself: I am love and wisdom; I am one with the universe. Exchanging a positive affirmation for a negative thought releases the negative energy, preventing it from building up and creating disease in your body and, in the process, constructing a new paradigm of reality.

People who have a positive outlook are healthier. In fact, a majority of people who are unhealthy have been proven to have had continuous negative thoughts and feelings and tend to surround themselves with others who have the same negative thought patterns.

When you change your inner thoughts, feelings, and attitudes, your outer experiences automatically change. One of my clients was always saying things like: I don't have enough money; no one will like me for who I am; my job sucks! He was a real mess and having a "pity party" for himself. I taught him how to hold the following images and beliefs in his mind: he is a beautiful person inside and out, he lives in a world of abundance, and his world will turn around. I told him to revise his words to statements of abundance. Instead of cussing, fretting, and complaining he started thinking and saying things like: I have plenty of money; people like me because I am kind; my job is challenging but interesting. Now he is a wealthy man with a thriving business, a beautiful wife and four healthy, happy children. He spreads the news of how thoughts and attitudes affect lives, and his favorite affirmation is: I aspire to be who I am and not who others think I should be.

II. *Cooperation and Forgiveness*

- *To Forgive = To "Give For"*
- *Substitute the Positive for the Negative*

Healing occurs when you remove negative thoughts from your mind and replace them with the belief you have perfection inside of you. Forgiveness is required to unplug your thought energy from past events and hurts.

Tension, fear, and anxiety affect your body because they block the natural flow of your life energy. As long as you hold on to destructive feelings you will remain unbalanced: you cannot be in harmony with life if you hold on to destructive and negative feelings and attitudes. Although it is hard to release old thought patterns and the negative people who are affecting your life, it is possible! Do the following;

- *Forgive*
- *Release*
- *Receive*
- *Cooperate*

Forgiveness means to give up, to release. Letting go of old hurts and emotional baggage releases you from the bonds of the past, and enables you to stop judging people and situations through the distorted lens of past experiences. For example, releasing the admonishing voice of your father calling you a "dummy" or saying you will never amount to anything allows your true spirit to emerge; now you feel confident and smart.

Eradicate destructive emotional attitudes by consciously developing the opposite constructive feelings. To forgive means to "give for." Instead of feelings of resentment, for example, show feelings of love and good will. Exert your conscious will to replace the negative with the positive, thus releasing negative energy from your mind, body, and spirit.

- *Exchange a negative for a positive, as follows:*
- *Fear for Faith*
- *Hate for Love*
- *Confusion for Composure*
- *Anger for Calm*
- *Dread for Elation*
- *Resentment for Forgiveness*

In releasing negativity, you must forgive all perceived wrongdoings. This frees your innate creative power so it can restore harmony to your life. When you feel anger or resentment toward someone, repeat this simple affirmation silently or out loud: " I forgive you (name), and I release you to the universe". After a time your anger and hurt will dissolve.

If you doubt this will work, try it the next time an inconsiderate driver cuts you off on the highway. Instead of cursing and making an offensive gesture, repeat out loud: "I forgive you, fellow driver. I release you to the universe". Instantaneously you will feel calm and relieved, and you will be able to stay focused on your driving.

To receive means to accept. Anything you can mentally accept you can have. Remember, your attitude is the only weapon that can harm you. Expecting "the best" works on all levels of your life and opens the path for increased health, wealth, and happiness.

Therefore, prepare yourself to receive abundance. For many people, this is the hard part. Some still hold the old idea that poverty and self-sacrifice are pleasing to God. You may believe God has finished His work and created all He can, and the majority of people must live in poverty because there is not enough wealth to go around; yet there is great abundance in the universe. We have been taught not to ask for wealth and to believe it is virtuous to stay poor. The truth is, our lives become rich through creation, and when you create spiritual wealth, myriad blessings will follow, including material wealth. Rid yourself of the old idea that God's wish is for you to be poor and unhappy, or you do not have the right to have the things you desire. It is God's desire for you to be rich in all areas of your life. Remember, you were created in God's image, one of total perfection. God lives in you and in everyone around you. God wants you to be the fullest possible physical expression of your spiritual self. So, make a conscious, conscientious effort to unlock your mind to be a receptor of only good things.

You must remove yourself from a competitive mindset, for there is never a need to act in haste or out of greed. No one will beat you to what you want; **there is always enough for all.** We make mistakes when we act hastily because we are acting from anger, doubt, or fear.

An attitude of cooperation invites accomplishment. Life flows through you automatically when you *stop resisting it*. Cooperate with yourself, with others, and with the power of God within you. To be a successful person you must learn to live life effortlessly; adjust to every situation and make the best out of it. Holding an attitude of cooperation allows you to do this.

III. Guidelines for Cooperative Living

Life was meant to be a joyful and peaceful experience, and you can choose to live free from fear. Say to yourself: I am fearless and I follow God's guidance. Cleanse and clear your mind of fear and anger so you can hear God's divine guidance. Envision your universe as a starburst of light advancing your life toward perfection and healthy functioning. Relieve your fears and dive into your spiritual nature to rediscover yourself from within.

Lynn's story shows how to choose to live free from fear. A young woman in her mid twenties, Lynn made the decision to seek counseling when her painful bouts with depression became debilitating. Shortly after she started having an affair with a married man, when traditional counseling did not bring her any relief, she sought spiritual counseling.

During our first session together Lynn told me she felt pressured to settle down, get married, and start a family. Her biggest fear was she would never meet the right man. In fact, her fear of not finding the right man led her every time to the wrong man! Each failed relationship was followed by a severe depression and this bout was the worst.

Unhappy with her job but not certain what else she wanted to do, Lynn was afraid to quit. The security of a regular paycheck was hard to let go of. Even though she had saved enough money to live on for awhile, she could not muster the courage to leave her job. Lynn was tired of feeling sorry for herself and wished she could make better use of her energies; yet, she was not able to determine what she should spend her time and effort on.

In the course of growing up and trying to make our way in the world we develop all kinds of ideas about who we are and who we think we should be, and the people and events in our lives influence the majority of our ideas. From the time we are born external forces affect and mold us: our parents, teachers, friends, and others push their expectations of how we should think, feel, and be. In Lynn's case, through many counseling sessions she began to discover she was not the person she wanted to be and she was struggling with several conflicting expectations. The source of her problems lay in her family of origin.

Lynn's mother was a devoted wife and mother who had given up her career aspirations. Although she had sensed her mother's resentment, Lynn developed the belief that in order to be successful and to be loved, she had to get married and have children. Through our work together Lynn realized she really did not want children and she had been attracting the wrong type of men into her life: men who were not available. Subconsciously she believed that a successful relationship meant she could not have a career; therefore, she was not willing to make any commitments, and, unknowingly, she sabotaged herself.

Lynn's father had been the family's main provider; he worked at the same job his whole life, six days a week, ten hours a day. He continued to provide a secure home life for his family even though he often came home angry and upset and rarely expressed any joy or sense of fulfillment regarding his job. Subconsciously Lynn believed work enjoyment did not accompany a secure pay check; hence, her inability to find the courage to change her job.

I showed Lynn to reconnect with her true self, encouraging her to remember things from her past that brought her joy and happiness, and then to concentrate on how that joy and happiness made her feel inside. Using creative imagery and focusing on what would make her happy, Lynn discovered that being in the arts would bring her joy. Previously, she could not summon the courage to follow her heart's desire because she sensed people around her did not want her to pursue an arts career. Lynn held in her mind the image that she was important, embracing faith that the universe was abundant and moving her toward happiness and it got her to the joyful place she now inhabits as a happy and successful artist.

Just like Lynn your personal experiences have shaped and molded you into what you have become and, unfortunately, experiences do not always inspire us to live a life that reflects who we really are. All too often we are persuaded by the fear of not being loved and accepted by others. Many of us make choices that do not comprise our true feelings, beliefs, and personal morals. If you are in the habit of making such choices, your individuality and uniqueness are buried, for it is not your true self that you are showing the world. In order to meet the demands and expectations placed on you by your peers, or in order to be loved and accepted, you wear the mask of the person you think you should be.

Living behind a mask invites feelings of anger, jealousy, depression, frustration, and loneliness; it precipitates addictions to drugs, food, sugar, alcohol, sex and gambling. You might find yourself disliking your job, your home and your life, yet you move unhappily along, convinced that somehow destiny is at hand. Sadly, the truth is you have come to identify yourself with the lie you are living and in the process have forgotten who you really are.

Unlocking your spirit to self discovery is about peeling off the layers of deception one by one to reveal the wonderful, perfect and loving individual you are. This is your true nature, your authentic self. Unlocking your true self can take honesty, trust, and perseverance, but all it takes to begin is an inkling of faith and courage. With a tiny spark of intention and with trust in yourself, your determination will become a beautiful roaring fire.

Remembering who you are is what unlocking yourself to find your true spirit is all about. Contrary to popular belief, it makes no difference what religious organization you do or do not subscribe to, because all paths have merit. You simply need to open your heart and let the universe guide you. Every mistake and challenge is an opportunity to grow, and in the process of learning to love yourself you will find the power to become what it is you envision for yourself.

This will take time, and it is the hardest work you will ever have to do. You must depend on no one but yourself. In the past you have looked to someone else, your parents, your spouse, or your friends, to define you. Do not let yourself lean on any one person or any one thing; support comes through many different channels.

To the many stay-at-home moms and wives who do not have their own income and feel they are less valued in our culture: yours is the most important job on earth. You have the grandest power, and your responsibility is the greatest because your children learn from you. There is nothing wrong with having one main breadwinner while one parent takes care of the home front. You, too, have the power to gain your desires through recognition of your subconscious mind, and the mental pictures you hold in your mind are just as sure to become real as those of your spouse who has a successful career.

Eventually you will recognize that true joy comes from your soul. You will stop choosing destructive behaviors that bring you harm, and you will choose peaceful ways for your life. Let go of fear, and let go of anger; for when you are full of fear and anger, your mind is not clear and you cannot receive guidance. Release aspects of your life that are not useful or good for you, like bad habits and destructive patterns. Nothing is lost through releasing them; instead, you eliminate error and negativity from your life and expand your virtue.

Train yourself to think of and look upon the world as something full of beauty and wonder, and do not let negative feelings impede your progress. Be careful what you say; never speak of yourself or anything in your life in a negative or discouraging way. Never admit the possibility of failure or speak of times being hard. Create what you want and, most of all, lose your fear!

Jesus lived his life in perfect harmony with body, mind and spirit and was sent here to be an example of how to live life. He lived by this set of rules:

- *Seek nothing*
- *Give everything*
- *Love all people*
- *Trust God*
- *Live each moment fully*

Here are my guidelines for living in harmony by following the example of Jesus.

- *Give from your heart.*

- *Keep your promises.*
- *Forgive those who offend you.*
- *Do what you love.*
- *Be enthusiastic.*
- *Smile.*
- *Associate with positive people.*
- *Ignore negative comments.*
- *Expect the best out of everything.*
- *Believe in yourself.*
- *Have faith in yourself in others.*
- *Be humble.*
- *Speak truth.*
- *Apologize when you are wrong.*
- *Maintain positive thoughts.*
- *Show appreciation.*
- *Find things that give you spiritual strength.*
- *Respect yourself and others.*
- *Choose to be better, but not better than others; rather be better than you were in the past.*
- *Choose to have more, so you can give more.*
- *Choose "knowing how" and "knowing why" so you can share your knowledge with others.*
- *Banish thoughts of competition from your mind and kindle thoughts of cooperation; you are here to create, not to compete for what has already been created.*

Hold a clear picture in your mind of what you want, then develop a conviction that it is already yours. You need to develop a conviction so your mind and heart know you can do whatever you want to do.

Only you can determine what your convictions should be. If you do not know what they should be, no one else will know either.

As you discipline your mind, you need to have expectancy. The answers to your prayers are in your attitude of expectancy and in your faith that what you want will become reality. But be sure what you are expecting is what you want to experience, because powerful forces are set in motion by your attitudes of expectation.

Condition yourself to expect good to come from everything. Tell yourself: "I look at all upcoming events with enthusiasm and the good for all". If you look for good you will find it, even if the upcoming moment or event looks unpleasant or unpromising. Because your external circumstances are a reflection of your inner attitude, it is important to train yourself to see what you would like to see.

Your soul speaks to you in feelings: listen and follow. Your feelings are the language of your soul, and your soul is the truth which is the highest religion. Remember: God does not test you; you test yourself.

Although this sounds easy to do, it is not. It is hard to release old thought patterns from the way you were brought up to believe. It is difficult to block out the negative voices and emotions of the surrounding people who are affecting or even poisoning your life. Yet with practice, anyone can succeed. Do this to clear your mental channels and let your spirit energy flow:

1. *Stop thinking about what is bothering you.*
2. *Get comfortable and think pleasant thoughts.*
3. *Visualize energy and positive emotions.*
4. *Know this energy is positive and a solid foundation for all good things in your life.*

Let go of your inner attitudes of fear, tension and pressure which aggravate an already existing weakness in your body. Replace fear with faith, doubt with certainty, suspicion with trust, inferiority with confidence, hate with love, guilt with forgiveness, violence with gentleness, irritation with pleasantness, confusion with peace, conflict with agreement, cruelty with kindness, and anxiety with serenity.

IV. Stay the Course

Once you have reached a decision, you must follow through. You have sent a thought into orbit; now you must go along for the ride. You have developed a strong conviction about what you want, and the powers of the universe are working to make it a reality: creative forces are working on it whether you are or not.

If you want to be healthy, wealthy, and happy, do not read or watch anything that pollutes your mind with gloomy images of scarcity and suffering. Those images will linger in your mind and be reflected in your day-to-day living. Keep positive images in your mind, for they will heal you and make you whole. Your positive desires will not bloom if you are watching, thinking, or reading about bad things.

The struggles you are experiencing today, the tensions, short tempers, and anxieties are the start of your inner change. Through your personal conflicts, you are becoming more aware and sensitive. Don't let today's difficulties jar you: hold steadily to this course of positive imagery and your life will begin to change.

Chapter 3:
Faith and Gratitude

Key 2: Nurture Faith Gratitude

I. Nurture Faith

Faith is the emotional attitude which says "yes" to life. Faith is like a muscle- the more you use it, the stronger it becomes and the more power you have to bring the virtue of your spirit into actuality. Faith is acting as though blessings are on the way even before you see evidence that this is so. Proclaim your blessings as if you already have them, even before you see their expression in your life. Remember, there is abundance for the person who will trust in the universe and go with the tide instead of trying to swim against it.

In order to nurture faith, you must have a relationship with God. There are 5 basic steps to have a relationship with God:

1) *Know God*
2) *Trust God*
3) *Love God*

4) Embrace God

5) Thank God

Your beliefs about God can either lead you to a limited existence or to accepting and claiming the best in your life. Lack of faith limits you. Believe there is unlimited goodness available to you. This frees you from limited beliefs and results in your life. Expect the best and live so that the best may become part of your experiences.

Doubt or disbelief is a certain way to start a negative pattern around you. When your faith wavers, you push away all that's good. Just as when you hold negative impressions in your mind, you block all the good that is coming your way. Every minute you spend worrying, every minute your spirit is clouded by disbelief, you set yourself on a current away from God.

Develop your faith in a Higher Being and realize that, like Dorothy who knew how to get back to Kansas from the Land of Oz, you have always had the answers inside of you. Have faith that the best will be done and that a Higher Power is working to fix your problems and to fulfill your desires. Stop worrying.

Keep developing your faith and beliefs. You cannot get positive results with a negative attitude, and you will never achieve anything when you believe you can't. Control what you think and feel and you will control your experience. For The Keys to be effective, your belief or faith is the most important element.

II. **The Gratitude Habit**

Life is better when you feel you are blessed, when you are able to look at your life and say, "Thank you, God" or "Thank you,

Universe." Whether or not you are religious, when you see your life as a great gift, you will absolutely experience a richer one.

Of course, it is easy to think gratitude comes from having what you want. You might imagine yourself giving thanks if you had more money, a loving, happy family, a vacation home, new car, etc. Yet, many people who possess these things are ungrateful and unhappy, and there are people with very little who are full of gratitude for all they have. So where does this feeling of gratitude come from?

An attitude of gratitude comes from how you look at things, from your perspective. It is the natural feeling that comes when you recognize the real value of the people and circumstances in your life. If you focus on the good in your life then you cannot help but have a better attitude and a better experience. Gratitude is something you can learn; it is an attitude you can nurture, encourage, and develop.

How can you be thankful for something you have not taken the time to even notice or enjoy? The first step is to "stop and smell the roses." Take some time to appreciate your world: your family, your comforts, your home, your friends, your job.

The second step is to make appreciation a life habit. You do not need to ignore the ugliness in the world; consciously choose to see the beauty and good in the world, and do this every day until it becomes automatic.

A good way to foster the gratitude habit is to write down every positive thing that has happened to you and all the things that bring you joy and make you smile. Every day write down at least one thing you appreciate; eventually you will automatically see all good things in your life. Have you ever bought a car and all of sudden you notice the same car everywhere? This is an example of how your awareness and your focus can alter your perception of reality. You didn't notice those cars before because you weren't paying attention to them. In the same way, once you are aware of the existence of good in the world and start looking for it, *paying attention to it*, you will see it everywhere.

Using these techniques, over time you can train your mind. When you are in the habit of counting your blessings, gratitude and a richer experience of life will be the results. Now you have the attitude of gratitude.

Lack of gratitude will prevent you from unlocking and accessing your life's treasure chest. Many people who live their life "right" in many ways still cannot find happiness and riches because they lack gratitude. Having received one gift from God, they cut the wires which connect them with Him by failing to make grateful acknowledgment. Gratefulness keeps you in close touch with God. The more gratefully you fix your mind to The Source when good things come to you, the more good things you will receive and the more rapidly they will come your way.

Jesus always had a grateful attitude. He always seemed to be saying, "I thank Thee, Father, that Thou hearest me." You cannot channel God's power without gratitude, for it is gratitude that keeps you connected with Divine Energy.

Having a mental attitude of gratitude draws the mind into closer touch with The Source, bringing your whole being into alignment with the creative energies of the universe. Gratitude alone can keep you close to The Source. It can prevent you from falling into an unhealthy way of thinking, for example, that the supply of abundance is limited. Thinking this way would be fatal to your hopes and dreams. One great lie is that we dwell in a world of scarcity; the truth is we live in a world of abundance. Another great lie is that we were born to struggle and must experience pain to grow. Remember these are other people's perceptions of life; all you need to do is to change yours.

Faith is born out of gratitude. The grateful mind continually expects good things, and that expectation becomes your faith. Give thanks continuously, and when giving thanks, recognize the presence of a Superior Power. Here are some rules to follow when expressing gratitude:

1) *Believe there is One Intelligent Source from which all things come;*
2) *Believe this Source gives you everything you desire;*
3) *Connect to The Source by feeling a deep and profound gratitude.*

Even though God wants nothing but good for each and every one of us, you should not have the idea of feeling entitled to whatever you desire. To free yourself spiritually and psychologically, eliminate the idea of entitlement from your life and embrace the attitude of gratitude.

In your thinking choose your brightest future, accept it as normal for you, expect it to happen, and then give thanks as if it has already happened. Be thankful and have faith that what you need will be done.

Gratitude enables you to experience God in a personal and powerful way. "Thank you" is the simplest and one of the most important prayers you can say every day, and using the key of gratitude will strengthen your faith and renew your purpose.

Chapter 4:
Mind Over Matter

Key 3: Think and Create

I. Focus Your Mind

Your thoughts, attitudes, and feelings are the "parents" of your experiences. By ordering and disciplining your mind, you can consciously create circumstances, produce conditions, and control your destiny. In fact, you have already subconsciously created the environment which you now inhabit.

You can consciously create circumstances, produce conditions, and control your destiny by ordering and disciplining your thoughts. You have choices:

1) You can let your uncontrolled thoughts create the moment.

2) You can allow your creative consciousness to create the moment, allowing a new idea from a higher source than your intellect can summon.

> *3) You can allow the collective consciousness to create the moment, allowing your conscious and subconscious mind to bring something to reality.*

Your thoughts determine the world you see and the life you live: happy thoughts will create happy feelings and experiences; negative ideas foster negative experiences. Through constructive thinking you can change the path of your life from negative to positive.

Consider Sally who was raised in a conservative middle class neighborhood. Her father died from a stroke when she was six years old and her mother never remarried. Sally's mother lived in fear and had a hard time trusting others; she was very insecure and did not have many friends. Feeling alone after her husband's passing, she focused all of her attention on raising Sally. As she got older Sally's mother put more responsibility on her to fill her father's shoes, looking to her daughter for strength, guidance, friendship and emotional support. A lot like her father, Sally was very independent, and as she got older, she did all she could do to avoid her mother. She found herself feeling uncomfortable around her mother and spent hours in her room painting, imagining herself as a famous artist.

Sally's mother, who had always resented her husband for spending time away from her in his workshop, criticized Sally's art work. She made Sally come out of her room to do chores just so she would have her company. As she got older the tension grew between Sally and her mother. Eventually she stopped coming home after school and hung out with her friends. In the eleventh grade, in order to fill a void of unhappiness and to release her stored-up anger, Sally ran with a group of tough kids who drank and vandalized property.

When Sally was seventeen years old her mother received a call from the police. When she found out Sally was being charged with underage drinking and that she and her friends had been driving a stolen car, she was in shock. Embarrassed, she told the police to keep her daughter in jail to teach her a lesson. After she was released from jail, Sally left home and moved to another state. Although this experience with the law helped her to straighten out, Sally could not be in her mother's company another minute because of her incessant criticism.

Many years passed before Sally decided to seek spiritual help. She told me she hated her job. She would like to settle down and get married; but she could not find Mr. Right. She was often short-tempered with friends and co-workers and experienced long spans of depression.

Over time Sally identified the "demons" inside of her. She began to recognize the many parts of herself which she had hidden away all these years. Sally went through a dark time when the grief of her father's death, the responsibility of filling his shoes, and the anger she felt toward her mother came to the surface. To expel her dark demon Sally needed to bring light into herself, and in order to do this she had to spend a lot of time alone. In her solitude she rediscovered her love for art and recognized artistic urges to create pottery. Sally found that the more comfortable she became exploring the darkness inside of her, the less she felt the pains of depression. She spent more time alone painting and creating beautiful pottery pieces. Her creative mind was at work helping to illuminate her spirit.

Through a series of "coincidences" or divine intervention, Sally was offered and accepted a job opportunity that involved using her creative ability. She was finally in her element. Sally eventually met a like-minded man and has found peace and happiness.

Sally was lucky she realized her depression was symptom of deeper underlying issues. She found the courage to take responsibility for her anger and depression and was not ashamed to ask for help. By poking into her soul and realizing it was full of darkness, she was able to uncover the key to her unhappiness. By taking the time to allow her emotions to resurface and honing the dark period this process invited, she released negative feelings and allowed them to bloom into wisdom. Too often it is our misunderstanding that harm comes from the negative emotions that we experience; harm comes to us only when we do not accept our real selves and from the blame we throw into the world for not allowing us to be what we feel we could be if the world would just let us.

Because you will tend to become like the things that surround you, your environment is very important in the process of identification. If there is beauty, you will feel beautiful; if there is anger you will feel angry; if there is hatred you will feel hateful. You have the power to choose what you will identify with. Because you are a thinker, you are a creator; therefore you live in a world of your own creation. Your thoughts have the power to produce tangible things like health, wealth, and happiness in your life, and they create and recreate everything you want or need, like a new job, love affair, good health, and monetary or spiritual wealth. When you know how to think you can create at will anything you need.

Conviction is the most important step in finding happiness and peace of mind. Remember, though, you still need to know what it is you want; you need to have a clear vision to bring it out in a tangible expression. Behind this purpose you must have an indestructible and unwavering faith the vision is already yours, it is "at hand," and you just have to take ownership of it.

God knows you have needs, and He knows before you even ask. You do not need to pray by repeating words. By holding your vision with unshakable faith and purpose you will attain it; always keep in your mind's eye the image of what you want to experience.

First, perform a mental house cleaning and throw away any garbage that clutters your mind. This garbage consists of things like doubt, worry, fear, or other people's opinions. Then, form a clear and distinct mental picture. Take the time every day to let this vision embed itself in your mind. Start each day with that clear picture, and expect what you visualize. Recognize wishing and wanting are not enough; wishing must grow into a faith that you accept internally. Quell any doubts with the realization that your current situation was *unconsciously* created by the same process that you are now *consciously* applying.

Your friends and family may not be excited about your dreams and ambitions; they may assail you with reasons why you should not be happy or do what it is that you want to do. Tune out their criticisms; hold to your purpose, forgive yourself, and, most importantly, trust yourself.

As a spiritual being in a human body, you do not and can not know everything; you make mistakes and think in error. In not knowing everything you believe in things that are not true. You hold ideas which cause disease and abnormal function and unhealthy conditions in your body and your life. Sick thoughts do not originate in God, for He never contemplates disease or imperfection. God does not give us heartaches and disease, poverty, or any of the world's problems; we give them to ourselves. The bad or imperfect things in your life were not created by God; they were created by your imperfect thoughts. Imperfect human beings create imperfect realities.

Because you began your life with imperfect impressions of yourself and your surroundings, you hold ideas of disease and abnormalities resulting from distorted views that others have instilled in you from birth. These thoughts and ideas have created the life you have. By altering your thoughts, you can re-create your life.

Your mind is a creative thinking center. Thoughts are energy; therefore, your thoughts are the most powerful tools you have. Everything is formed from thoughts. By thinking imperfect thoughts you cause imperfect functions; thoughts of disease produce physical forms of disease. Thoughts of poverty and imbalance can cause real scarcity and disparity in your life.

If you are a thinking center who creates all you need with thoughts, through thinking imperfect thoughts you create imperfect functions in your body and in your life. If follows, then, that your life can be improved by thinking and feeling in a certain way. Your feelings are not meant to get you in trouble. Your feelings are your truth. Knowing your truth will free your spirit and invite blessings into your life.

There is a Thinking Stuff from which all things are formed. Thoughts are energy that produce the things being thought of. You can form things just by thinking of them, but in order to achieve this you have to live in full harmony with God by living a sincere and thankful life. You can live a joyous and fulfilled life on the creative plane by uniting yourself with God through a deep and continuous feeling of gratitude.

II. **Hold the Vision**

Let your vision develop in your mind; see it, feel it, and live it. Set a beleif of already having what you envisioned, then act from that viewpoint. If you expect the right things they will come to you. If are troubled, stop thinking about the trouble and think of God instead. There is no limit to the power of God. When you think of God instead of your problems, the problems disappear. Set aside your analytical mind and allow your consciousness to go beyond the realm of the unknown into what you formerly saw as impossible to create. With trust, set out on the journey to unlock your life, beyond what you knew as possible.

Stop changing your mind. Maintain a clear picture of what you desire; have patience and be persistent.

III. Think and Create

Because you are a center of thought and creativity, you must keep your thoughts perfect, because by thinking imperfect thoughts you cause defective functions. Unhealthy thoughts are not of God. God, The Source, never makes us think or create unhealthy things. God thinks nothing but health and good things! Since God lives within you, you should only be thinking healthy, clean, and positive thoughts.

You can change and heal your life by thinking in a certain way. Two essential ways are by having faith and by the personal way you apply it your life. Start thinking God is good, life is worthwhile and rewarding, and you are richly blessed. Deliberately picturing the good you want draws it to you. God works with your thoughts and needs by attracting the appropriate people and circumstances to help you get what you want. God provides amazing channels of good for you.

Many people feel they cannot change their world. The opposite is true: if you do not like your world or the people in it, you can change it by changing your thoughts. Just like drawing on an Etch-a-Sketch you can create and recreate pictures over and over, but the pictures are different every time. Keep doing this until you get the picture you want your life to be.

Think like this: My *mind is clean, and I am thinking clearly. As I relax, my negative emotions are leaving and positive ones are flowing. I feel love toward all people and toward myself. I am able to accomplish all tasks with endless energy.* Focus your mind and the creative power within you forms the physical image of that which you give your attention to.

This affirmation gets your thoughts flowing in the right direction:

I am good. God exists in me and I exist in God.

Through conviction I become what I am meant to be.

I am strong. I am true. I am whole.

This conviction emanates from my spirit. I am one with God. It is so.

Use your mind to form mental images of what you want. Hold that vision with faith and purpose, and use your willpower to keep your mind moving in the right direction. Your will determines which things your attention stays focused on.

First form a clear and definite image of what it is you want; you cannot send forth the image if you do not have a clear vision of it. Think of your mind as a movie screen upon which you project what it is you desire.

If you were going to send a text message to a friend, you would not send the letters in alphabetical order and then let the receiver make up his own message. Nor would you send random words and let him construct his own message. You would send a message that means something. When you express your wants and desires to

God, remember to have *clear intentions*: you must know what it is you want and be definite about it. Mentally review your wants and desires, visualize what it is you want, and develop a clear picture in your mind *as you wish it to look when you receive it*. Hold that clear mental picture continually in your mind; keep your mind focused toward it all the time, and don't lose sight of it.

To be able to form a clear mental image of the things you desire, you must pass from the competitive mind to the creative mind. With steady intention hold this picture in your mind. To get what you want you need to have unwavering faith that will bring about what it is you desire. Keep your mind fixed with faith and the purpose of the vision of what you want.

So here is the plan: once you have a clear vision formed, make an oral statement, address God in prayer, and from that moment you must in your mind receive what you are asking for. Live in the new house, see yourself in a loving relationship, or set sail on a new career. Hold to the faith that what you imagine is being realized, and hold to the purpose to realize it.

IV. *The Power of Intention*

Focus your attention on the very best for yourself and surround yourself with excellence. Do not waste time thinking or talking about the shortcomings in your life. Use your willpower to keep your mind off the subjects of poverty, war, illness, etc. Visualize a clear picture of what you want and a certain concept of what you want to do, have, or become. Hold onto those images and do not lose sight of them. When you believe in abundance rather than in the scarcity, you will always have plenty.

Your intention is a powerful tool that can be used in a positive manner, or it can be used to hurt if incorrectly applied. When properly employed, your own personal power has amazing, positive benefits. Accept and take responsibility for what you create, and dedicate yourself to a meaningful purpose.

Never apply your will to anyone outside of yourself; not to a friend, spouse, your children, or anyone else. You have no right to impose your will on anyone other than yourself, because your will for others might not be the same as their will for themselves. It is wrong to apply your will to affect others for your personal growth. This applies even when you are praying for someone's healing or good fortune, because it must be their own will for something to change in their life. Do not spend time asking God to answer others' prayers; they need to ask for themselves. Even if you have good intentions, you would be robbing a person of their personal choice. What you intend for someone's benefit may ultimately not serve their purpose; therefore, you should never use willpower on another even if you perceive it is for their own good. Any use of your will on others defeats your purpose, which is to use your willpower for your own personal growth and happiness.

When you know what to think and do, you must use your will to compel yourself to think and do the right things. Use your willpower to keep yourself from acting in a negative way; keep focused and positive.

It is imperative that you guard your thoughts, for now you know your beliefs will be shaped into the things you think about and consciously attend to. Things are not brought into existence by pondering their opposites. Thoughts in the spirit world are immediately manifested; in the physical, thoughts also become things, but it is a slower process. The chair you are sitting in was once a thought form, but now it has been translated into the physical. The physical is made of a much slower vibration than that of God's spirit so it takes more energy and effort for things to manifest in your physical life. Now here is where your unwavering intention comes into play, for it is by your willpower that you shape your life, that you determine what you want and what kind of life you will live. Be assured the world you live in is the product of your thoughts, both positive and negative. When you permit your mind to linger in dissatisfaction about things as they are, you begin to lose ground. If you focus your attention upon the unhealthy, the poor, and the bad, your mind takes the form of these things. Unknowingly you transmit these mental images to the formless realm, and the unhealthy, poor, and bad are what come back to you.

Good habits are the key to all successes, and bad mental habits block the door to success. Form positive habits and become a slave to them. Bad habits must be destroyed to pave the way for good ones. Failure will never overtake you if your determination to succeed is strong enough. Make a promise to yourself that nothing will stop your new life's growth.

Remember to clearly visualize the image of what you want to be. With God all things are possible; there is nothing you cannot accomplish, whether it is health, wealth, or anything in between.

Chapter 5:
An Invitation to the Divine

Key 4: Pray

I. Welcome God

Prayer is an invitation to welcome God into your life. Most people believe they must meditate in order to summon the power of prayer. In fact, every word that comes out of your mouth, every thought, every feeling is a prayer, and a prayer is always answered. When you speak, think, feel, and pray from your heart, mind, and spirit, it is communicated to God. Prayer is a conscious, intentional contact with the Supreme Power.

Prayer occurs any time and any place: at work, in your car, in the store while shopping, in bed before going to sleep, or when you wake up in the morning. True prayer is visualization that addresses specific problems and personal needs by allowing us to implement God's will in the physical dimension. When you pray fix in your mind and clearly visualize what it is you want, suspending all doubts. You must be in a receptive state of mind, open to Spirit. When you open yourself up to God, you will be filled with wisdom, counsel, health, and all you need in your life. Prayer is not to ask God to do something, but to be open to let God inspire you to act in his place, to enact His Will on earth. Prayer, therefore, is surrender; it is falling back into the arms of the Divine Spirit that lives inside of you. There are many ways to pray, but it is merging with God's Energy that is important. To ask God to provide something you think you do not have is the lowest form of prayer. Remember: God's will is your will; be mindful in creating the world around you.

The power of prayer stands on your intentions. Focus on your prayer already being answered, not on the chance of it being ignored. Prayer is never about the words you speak; it is about the conviction with which you express the words, and without love, no matter how beautiful the prayer, it is empty and useless. Effective prayers are infused with love.

Prayer dissolves fear and affirms faith. Prayer is your way to talk to God by making your prayers exactly that, a conversation! Speak, think, and feel; pray from your heart and mind. Carry on conversations with God through prayer during your everyday routines.

II. How to Pray

Affirmations are the simplest form of prayer. An affirmation is a grouping of words repeated to oneself daily, silently or spoken out loud, which stirs up the spark of Spirit within to initiate changes in outward manifestations. Affirmations are instigated by the conscious mind but aimed toward your subconscious mind to change your belief system, to bring your truth into being for any aspect of your life, such as harmony, balance, abundance, health, education. Your words do not need to be lengthy but they need to come from your heart. In essence, the prayer of affirmations lies not in the words or in some attitude of righteousness or arrogance but in your focus on God and on God's attributes as if they were your own. What you believe about God is the most important thing about you, and your belief or the lack of it translates into your actions and attitudes.

Desire is the irresistible urge toward expression of your spirit. It is perfectly fine to pray for anything you desire as long as it is constructive and in no way contradicts the unity of your spirit. Again, focus on your prayers being answered, not on the chance of them being ignored.

If your prayers usually begin with "Lord, help me," stop for a moment and see if you can turn your prayer into an affirmative statement: *Dear God, I know I have the strength to face the difficulties of this day. You fill me with inspiration and wisdom to resolve any problems that may come up.*

Do not use repetition when praying. It is best to use your own words, not the words of others. Speak, think, and feel prayer from your own heart and mind. Your every thought and feeling is a prayer, and a prayer is always answered. Never hesitate to ask on a large scale, but remember to focus and express your desires to God.

Many of us have been taught prayers that had little or no positive effect. What is wrong with the prayers you learned as a child or in church? Why aren't those verses the prayers you should be saying? If God was sitting around waiting to answer your prayers, would He want to hear the Our Father or Hail Mary repeated 40 times with none of your own personal words spoken from your heart telling of your needs and desires? Or would God like for someone to speak to Him with true words full of feelings and love from the heart?

III. *Leave It To God*

Many people give up on praying because they do not get what they want or need. Prayer does not work for some people, because praying is not to ask God to do something but to open the door to let God inspire us to act in His Place to enact His Will on earth, for we are emissaries of the Divine.

When you stop obsessing and complaining to God you leave problems in His Hands, and He shows you the way to solve them. That is not just wishful thinking; it is a belief based on the sacred truth that God wants you to live in joy and abundance. For example, if you are having chronic financial difficulties and have been complaining to God about your lack of money, focus on the problem in a positive way to set prayer in motion. You might say: *I know, God that your desire is to see me prosper in all areas of my life. Right now I open my being to receive prosperity.* When you center yourself on God rather then obsessing about your personal difficulties or problems, God reveals Himself as a genuine presence, a living vibrating energy that lives inside of you.

Carry on conversations with God every day. Build expectancy though prayer. Blessings come when you hold an attitude of expectancy and faith when you pray. Prayer should be affirmative.

Use these affirmations to fill up with goodness and abundance:

- Everything I need I have. Everything I need comes to me. Everything I need is revealed to me.

- God, I know you give me strength to face any difficulties of the day. You fill me up with inspiration, love, and wisdom to resolve any problems that appear.

- I know, God that it is Your desire for me to prosper in all areas of my life. Right now I am open to receive Your prosperity.

- I am relaxed in my mind. My mind is clean and I am thinking clearly. As I relax, my negative feelings are leaving and positive ones are flowing. I feel love toward myself and all people. I accomplish all tasks with endless energy.

- I am relaxed and at peace with my world. I am in perfect harmony with myself and others. I am at ease with my life at all times. I am thankful and it so.

- I am one with every living thing. I am one with the Creator. Abundance surrounds me. There is a steady stream of light flowing though me that flows from the One Source.

You cannot impress God by having a special day set aside to tell Him what you want and then forgetting Him the rest of the week, or by having special hours to pray, especially if you then dismiss the matter from your mind until the hour of prayer comes again. You do not need to have an "hour of prayer," you need to pray without ceasing, that is, holding steadily to your vision with the intention to cause its creation in solid form and the faith that it is becoming so.

Once you have attained peace and happiness, you will be much less concerned about praying for what you want but more interested in what you need for fulfillment as a whole person.

Remember, affirmations are a form of prayer. Try these:

- Nothing is too good to be true.
- Nothing is too wonderful to happen.
- Nothing is too good to last.
- I am one with every living thing. I am one with the Creator. Abundance surrounds me. A stream of light flows through me; it flows from One Source, the fountain of all life.
- I love this Source which is God, the Infinite Intelligence. God loves me.
- I am success.
- I am health.
- I am happiness.
- I am freedom.
- I am prosperity.
- Good, better, best: I will never rest until my good is better and my better is best!

Identify with these concepts and they will be manifested in your life.

Prayer is one of the most powerful tools available to you. Through prayer, even the most impossible changes can occur. Medical studies have concluded that prayer really does help in the healing of disease.

If I were to ask others to define what prayer is, most would say it is talking to God and requesting his intervention. This definition is as good as any that I have heard. However, this raises a question. We accept as religious faith that God hears all prayers, yet why does He not seem to answer all of them? Some prayers are trivial compared to others, such as, God, please let my team win this game, or please let me win the lotto. Other prayers are most sincere, like, please heal my sick child. Many of these sincere prayers go unanswered.

The faithful will always be willing to accept their prayers not being answered by saying that whatever happens is God's will and it was "for the best." Those of you who are religious always believe this to be true, no matter what the circumstances. Yet, prayer is not a request list for God: God, give me this, and God, give me that. An immature attitude towards prayers prevents them from being answered.

If you view prayer as a simple wish list, then you lack the necessary conviction for prayers to open the gates of the heavens and demand they be heard. The secret to successful prayer lies in your *intention*. In order for your prayers to be answered, you have to *mean* what you pray; the mere recitation of words *without intent* is not enough. There are many teachings on how prayer works, but is the level of your devotion during the reciting of the words you pray that makes prayer work.

When you pray, you must place all the power in the words you recite. When you speak about anything remember that your thoughts are radiated though your speech. Take care in your thoughts before putting them into your prayers. When you pray without first thinking about it, you are sending an incomplete image to God. The lines of communication are not clear and open because your unclear thoughts produce interference that blocks and distorts the message.

Prayer, thought, and speech all go together, and from your speech comes your actions. Thought is to speech what soul is to body. Every word you speak is important; that is why you must use care when praying or talking. When you waste your words with idle speech you are wasting your life force energy.

Chapter 6:
Putting It Together

I. Failure Is A Lesson

Your inner consciousness determines your outer experience, and your thoughts, attitudes and feelings are the parents of your experiences. You can consciously create circumstances, produce conditions, and control your own destiny by having a disciplined mind, because thought produces the thing that is imaged by the thought.

Your thoughts are energy which causes the creative powers within to act; thinking in a certain way will bring to you what it is you desire in a way you have never imagined. Retain your vision of what you would like, stick with the purpose, and maintain faith and gratitude. Your thoughts and personal actions combined help you attain your vision. The things you want are drawn to you by both the thoughts and actions you choose.

Seek knowledge, instruction, and advice about a specific thing, but never ask permission of others whether you should or should not pursue a course of action. Go ahead with it even if you make mistakes. Remember, failure may be a valuable lesson to you, perhaps more valuable than what you perceive as success. You need to feel the *total* experience in order to own it. Do whatever is necessary to achieve your goals, just be sure not to hurt anyone in the process.

We are given many choices. Know there are only "right" choices from which to choose. Although it might seem as though you have chosen a "wrong" road, your soul may have needed the detours and potholes along the way for a specific experience. Although the road may be bumpy, all roads lead to fulfillment.

II. Live In The "Now"

Live life in the "now" or the "present", for you cannot act in the past. It is essential to the acuity of your mental vision to dismiss the past from your mind. Residue from the past can cloud your mental vision – release it from your mind. Furthermore, you cannot act in the future because it is not yet here. Put your whole mind into the present action and do today's work with your best effort! View the "present" as a gift.

Because you are new at this and not an expert, you will at times hit walls. Have faith and keep trying! When you study with regular and daily discipline, applying yourself to "at-one-ment" with the One Source, you will be ready and prepared for anything that comes your way.

If you find yourself in a situation that does not feel "right" to you, whether at work, at home, or at school, take action before it takes over your life. Don't sit around and wait for something or for someone else to change: this is where *you* do the changing. Hold the vision of what you want and have faith that the right situation is moving toward you. Your clear vision of the "right" thing happening combined with your faith will cause the Supreme Being to move the appropriate situation toward you. Your focused intentions will guide you to a more fulfilled life.

A number of people believe through their religion that if they do something wrong or commit a "sin" God will punish them. These same people have had their faith shattered when something "bad" happens in their life; they feel like God is punishing them for something they must have done. Because they do not understand, they turn away from God when they need God the most. When you add the idea that if you do something wrong God will punish you to the idea that fate dictates the events in your life, the picture can be pretty upsetting: now you are being punished for doing things that you have no control over. It is not surprising we have a world of depressed and unhappy people.

I have some good news and some bad news. The good news is that the myths about destiny and fate are not true. It is time for you to take control over your life. You are not only in control of your present life; you are in control of your future as well. You live in a "free will" universe. Life without free will would be like a gift with strings attached; for example, if I gave you a TV but with the condition that you can only watch it when you are with me and only what I want to watch.

God does not punish you when you make a mistake. On the contrary, this is how you grow, learning from the choices you make. When you make a poor choice it will take you down a path of learning and growing which will help you make better choices in the future. If you do not learn from your mistakes, you will repeatedly make the same mistakes. Because God wants you never to stop growing He offers many opportunities to get it right. You will always be presented an opportunity to choose more wisely.

III. *Choose Your Life*

When you came in to this life you entered with certain tasks which include the opportunity to experience certain things. Karma is the law of action, for every action there is a reaction "good" or "bad" you might have debts to pay to others. You might have to experience helplessness, poverty, great love, or compassion, or any of a million possible scenarios.

All things in your life exist because you chose them. One of the hardest things to accept is that only you have the power to change your life. Sometimes when you feel you have the answers, you may try to save others from the pain of going through the consequences of their wrong choices. You cannot accept the responsibility for anyone else's choices and you certainly should not make their choices for them. To attempt to take over someone else's life is to rob them of the opportunity to learn their lessons. Many people are happier to let others live their lives for them and make all their decisions for them while hiding their heads in the sand; but that is the safe and easy way out, so when things do not go right they have someone else to blame. The problem with trying to rescue others from heartache and difficult times is that you do not know what experiences are essential for their spirit to advance and grow in earthbound life.

You are the master of your own future. Regardless you may experience things you would rather not go though. Accept responsibility for attracting what you experience and learn from it.

So what is the bad news? The bad news is also good news if you are willing to accept the challenge of living life. You can no longer play the "blame game"; it is not God's fault, your husband's, the devil's, or your mother's. The choices you've made are your own, and they've caused the situation you're in. The challenges you face are the challenges you have chosen. You will succeed in facing and overcoming them; you can find happiness within yourself.

You are growing as you experience the free will universe. You are living the life you are because you have chosen it. Celebrate the choices you have made. If you keep your heart open, they will bring you many opportunities.

Some will find this news the most difficult to accept while others will embrace it. What is the news? You are responsible for the life you lead and for translating what you believe into action. Take charge of your life and celebrate the wonderful gift you have been given. You are eternal and privileged to have the gift of a physical existence. How will you use it?

Chapter 7:
Choosing Happiness

I. Embrace Your Emotions

The search for happiness is a basic human desire. Influenced by your culture and social mores, you seek happiness through material possessions and worldly achievements. But as you grow wiser and more spiritually aware, you come to realize that the pursuit of happiness is not the key to living a life free of suffering and that suffering is not an all-encompassing evil.

Happiness, anger, depression, and grief are common human emotions, and contrary to what we sometimes believe, they are not diseases. The problem is that in many cultures we have been taught to ignore certain emotions. We have been conditioned to suppress our feelings for fear another person will not accept the way we think, feel, or act. However, everything you think and feel is a reflection of who you are, and as you begin to accept both the light and the dark aspects of yourself you will realize that happiness is not very different from sadness. Both are human emotions that serve to help you realize your true self. Instead of trying to escape your negative tendencies, let go of your embarrassment of being alive and human.

When I was a teenager, I babysat a well-behaved little boy named Jeffrey. In the afternoons Jeffrey and I spent our time making forts out of couch cushions and blankets; he would bring in his favorite toys and we would play until his parents came home. One day I noticed that his favorite stuffed animal was not in the fort, so I asked Jeffrey why he left out Charlie. In a stern voice Jeffery explained that Charlie was not allowed in the fort because he was in a bad mood, and when he decided to calm down he could come into the fort and play. Jeffrey had discovered that expressing anger, sadness and frustration displeased his parents; subconsciously Jeffrey learned that, in order for his parents to be happy, he had to be happy. In an attempt to avoid being punished and feeling responsible for his parents' happiness, Jeffery made the choice to refrain from expressing his negative emotions. In this way, disapproving parents like Jeffrey's inadvertently condition their children to suppress negative feelings.

Angela, a young woman I counseled, remembers a different approach her parents took to "keeping her quiet." Whenever she was upset or angry either her mother and grandmother fed her junk food or her father bought her toys. It is no wonder that when she came to see me she was morbidly obese and addicted to shopping. Thanks to her childhood conditioning, the only way she knew to cope with her negative feelings was to eat or spend money.

Addictions to sugar, food, cigarettes, drugs, sex, and shopping are a few of the more common addictions that people unconsciously develop when they do not know how to deal with their emotions. In Angela's case she was very comfortable being happy and excited, but when something made her feel unhappy, sad, or negative she would panic. In an attempt to remain composed she ate junk food or went on a shopping spree, effectively swallowing and suppressing her emotions. These methods provided only temporary fixes, and over time Angela's dependency worsened. The more she fought to hide her true self, the harder her true self fought to be expressed. Through our work together Angela has learned to accept who she is, to permit herself to experience both happy and unhappy feelings, and to stop allowing others to define how she lives her life.

Although you have been programmed and encouraged to suppress your negative emotions and expressions, it is not parents or other adults in your life who are to blame. They, too, were once children who where influenced by their family and the culture in which they grew up. Blaming others for your problems drains you of the power you have to make changes. The work must begin now, in this moment, with yourself. Only when you give yourself permission to be exactly who you are, when you are able to recognize the beauty and love in all the different aspects of your self, will you begin to see the beauty and joy in every moment.

II. *Stop Passing Judgment*

Joy is much more likely to engulf you when you let go of fear, anger, self pity and resentment; and you will be more likely to treat others with love and respect. Consider the wisdom in this poem:

The Cold Within
~Anonymous

Six humans trapped by happenstance
In the dark and bitter cold,
Each one possessed a stick of wood or so the story's told.

Their dying fire in need of logs
The first woman held hers back.
For the faces around the fire
She noticed one was black.

The next man looking cross the way
Saw one not of his church,
And could not bring himself to give
The fire his stick of birch.

The third one sat in tattered cloths
He gave his coat a hitch,
Why should his log be put to use
To warm the idle rich.

The rich man just sat back and thought
Of the wealth he had in store,
And how to keep what he had earned
From the lazy, shiftless poor.

The black man's face bespoke revenge
As the fire passed from sight,
For all he saw in the stick of wood
Was a chance to spite the white.

The last man in this group
Did naught except for gain,
Giving only to those who filled his purse
Was how he played the game.

The logs held tight in death's still hands
Was proof of human sin,
They did not die from the cold without
They died from THE COLD WITHIN.

You know this coldness, and you have felt its unforgiving bite. You have, at some time, felt its chill freeze your heart. The Cold Within is insidious, for not only does it cause people to suffer injustice, hate, and intolerance, but it propagates those very qualities in its victims. Feeding endlessly on itself, it causes people to react and behave in ways they despise in others. Although we have been warned to "Do unto others as you would have them do unto you," the coldness in our nature overrules our better judgment.

There are many names for The Cold Within: prejudice, intolerance, injustice, but no matter what you call it, it is wrong because it divides and separates people. A darkness that obscures the light, it kills the mind and limits the spirit, allowing people to view others as if they have a lesser spiritual value. People have a tendency to judge others, not necessarily though awareness but though ignorance. In passing judgment on others we avoid looking at ourselves. History has shown that those who judge are themselves eventually judged; choosing to believe everyone else is wrong does not make you right.

In a loving world, individual differences make each person special. Unfortunately, we tend to fear these differences in others because we do not understand them. Have you suffered because you were perceived as different, or because you did not share the same beliefs as others? There are groups of people all around the world who think others who disagree with their beliefs are inferior, crazy, evil or dangerous. We can share our views and opinions without presenting ourselves as superior to those who do not share the same ideas. Respect and accept people's differences without judgment.

This is the way to eliminate intolerance and injustice. Terrorist are an extreme manifestation of fear and intolerance. Check out our streets, playgrounds, classrooms, and workplaces and you will find a very similar dynamic among these groups. We must invest our time learning about others' views and customs. Appreciating people's uniqueness. Unfortunately, we tend to fear what we do not know or understand.

Stop judging, criticizing, and persecuting yourself and others. Let your heart open up and free your spirit to experience the natural joy and gratitude of being alive. When you learn to enjoy life you will have more confidence in yourself, work more efficiently, make more money, attract more friends and be far healthier than those who constantly abuse their bodies, have little self esteem, fight with others and live in fear. Starting today, simply by changing how you view the world, you can have a more fulfilling experience and optimal health:

- *Wear a smile on your face.*
- *See the beauty all around you.*
- *Take a deep breath instead if criticizing someone.*

☞ *Count to ten when you feel frustrated.*

☞ *Take a walk instead of throwing a verbal or physical punch.*

Lighten up and allow your life to intertwine with the buzz and beauty of nature. Do birds worry if spring will arrive on time? Do flowers fret that the snow will keep them hidden in the ground? Is rain troubled about whether it will have room to flow when it falls into the river? Do the sun and moon fight about which one is better or brighter? Enjoy the palette of a rainbow; the brushstrokes of clouds; the jingle of raindrops. Smile when you see someone; say hello to a new employee; help a stranger find his way; slow down and appreciate each moment. Greet each day with a sense of wonder and expectation of beautiful things. Before long, instead of sadness and anger you will see love and joy.

Reducing your stress requires the willingness to appreciate everything around you and in nature, to see what most are too busy to notice. See beauty, peace, and abundance in all that is and grows around you. The choice is yours and only yours. The rest of your life is waiting for you. Choose happiness.

Chapter 8:
Using the Keys at Work

I. Seek Good

Whether you are a business owner or an employee, you can use The Keys in the workplace. When you apply the keys in your work environment, you must look for the good in every person. Start with the way you perceive others. Write a success plan for the workplace including what you value and who you are. Focus on these ideas:

- Fulfilled people function best
- Exceptional quality
- Exceptional service

Deal with people fairly; it will benefit your spirit tenfold. When you know that you are doing right by others you are rewarded in countless ways. Remember, you reap what you sow.

Use creativity, laughter, and freedom to improve your employees' or coworkers' productivity. Creativity is a natural and healthy characteristic of humans. Applying creativity helps you see things in a different light. This allows you to break out of bad habits and shed light on a new way of thinking, doing, and being. When you hinder creativity, you lead yourself and your employees down a road of repression and negativity. When you are being creative you bring a sense of fun and spirituality to your work. When people enjoy what they do, productivity increases.

II. Foster Cooperation, Not Competition

Use communication as a vessel encouraging employees to work together. Most people have a hard time communicating because of how they were brought up and usually hide their feelings so they do not get in trouble with their parent, teacher, etc. In school, most did not learn to work together as a team. We were always competing against other students to get a better grade and earn the favor of the teacher.

As they enter the working world, many adults have not learned to communicate with their peers for the purpose of achieving something helpful for all. They have not learned to work together as equals. They try to win the acceptance of a "parent" or "teacher," usually a management figure. Often employees avoid speaking their minds or sharing their ideas and feelings for fear of retribution and disappointment. Consequently, employees try to figure out how to say the "popular thing," beat the system, and gain extra favors. They withhold creative ideas rather than risk "making waves" expressing their true opinions.

These old patterns manifest into the lack of respect for peers, employees, and even customers. Lack of respect for and acceptance of others leads to conflict and hostility which destroys businesses and the personal livelihood of many families.

Nurturing feelings of power and dominance over others will draw negativity into your life. It is the competitive not the creative mind at work. You can have control over your environment or your destiny without exercising power over others. Start thinking ***"What I want for myself, I want for everyone."***

Whether in a personal or work relationship, one of the most important skills to have is good communication. Ineffective communication leads to confusion, unnecessary conflicts, anxiety and mistrust, shutting people down and striking a devastating blow to productivity. Clear communication, however, leads the way to clarity, peace, trust and creative ideas and improved productivity.

Respect yourself and others, including the environment, other people's privacy, their different points of view, philosophies, religion, gender, lifestyle, ethnic origin, physical ability, beliefs, and personalities.

III. Expand Your Vision

Successful leaders and entrepreneurs have the vision to see beyond the obvious; they see the unseen. Where does this vision come from? For some, it is a natural trait. They have always had it and can see things others cannot. Others learn to expand their perspective and strive to follow a dream. They have a vision and hold in their minds what can be and the wealth of possibilities. They believe it is theirs and they "go for it." They follow their vision and let nothing impede their progress, whether obstacles or pessimists.

Vision can be learned. The only requirement is your strong desire to open yourself and expand your vision beyond your current sight path.

What are the most significant contributions you can make to your business?

- *Stay positive*
- *Be creative*
- *Communicate well*
- *Respect your employees*
- *Adapt to change*
- *Work well with others*
- *Enjoy what you do!*

Create positive energy around yourself. Believe positive energies surround you and attract success to all business endeavors, large or small. Positive energy forces are culminated when people are creative and have the freedom to express their opinions, when they feel respected by management and peers.

Staying positive can be a challenging undertaking. When we are surrounded by negative coworkers, friends, or even partners, it takes a strong conscious resolve to not get sucked into the void of negativity around you. *You can do this*; focus on how *you* are viewing your own situations.

- *Creativity helps to broaden your perspective. It allows you to break away from old habits.*
- *Clear communication helps build confidence and trust among fellow employees.*
- *Respect for your employees improves morale.*
- *Adapting to change is key as the world is rapidly evolving. Welcome change and adapt, allowing your own beliefs and habits to transform as necessary.*

The importance of working well with others can't be overstated. It's better to say nothing than to feed into others' negativity. Negative energy in the workplace creates a hostile environment which promotes dysfunction and counter-productivity.

Enjoy what you do! If you don't like what you are doing, visualize what you want to be doing and attract it to you.

In the workplace and in your personal life, your attitude about the world determines how your life will unfold. Make a choice today to live the fullest life possible, filled with friends and an enjoyable work environment.

IV. Strategies For Business Owners

If you want to run a successful business; if you want to experience a harmonious workplace; if you want to have abundance in your career, remember:

- People buy from people they trust.
- People buy from people who are caring and positive.
- People buy from people who take the time to listen.
- People buy from people who pay attention to details.
- People buy from people who are honest and make good on their promises.
- People buy from people who have a good value for the price.
- People buy from people who are a positive resource for them.
- People buy from people who promise a lot and deliver more.
- People buy from people take who pride in themselves.

Keep the following in mind:

- You are a creative center from which abundance flows.
- Focus on the thought of abundance no matter how small the job or transaction.
- Protect the natural environment.
- Nurture human creativity.
- Serve your higher purpose, including spiritual, service, and community values.
- Behave ethically.

For ages, many countries have fought devastating wars to attempt to prove their ways of thinking were better than others. They sought to acquire more power for themselves, rather than abundance for all. Unfortunately, the business world is much the same: people waste the lives and hearts of millions for money and power over others. Do not try to seek power over others. The desire to have power over others is both a selfish gratification as well as a curse that will diminish and ultimately destroy you.

No matter who you are or where you work, you *can* contribute to the abundance of yourself and others. Be an example of faith and purpose. Show others how to apply The Keys through your example.

Chapter 9:
Affirmations

I Effective Affirmations

Affirmations are powerful and positive statements of acceptance you will use to allow the manifestation of your destiny. In order for affirmations to be effective, *you must hold as an unwavering belief you can create your destiny.* There is no place for wishy-washy attitudes such as, "Well, maybe I'll try it out and see if works." With each affirmation you must visualize it as reality. For example, along with your affirmation of "I am calm, I am quiet, I am peaceful," hold in your mind's eye a picture of yourself *being* calm, quiet, and peaceful, perhaps relaxing in a hammock under swaying palm trees on a tropical beach. Or, with your affirmative statement of "I am graduating from college in May of next year," visualize yourself walking up to the platform and then accepting your diploma from the school's president. Another example: As you repeat the words, "I can control my anger today," envision yourself responding calmly to a typical trigger. Let's say your usual response to being cut off in traffic is to curse vehemently while seething with anger. Hold a vision of yourself responding in a different way, perhaps smiling as you take a deep breath, then releasing the negativity and anger from your body as you exhale.

Remember, every thought is a prayer; God hears your thoughts whether you are "officially" praying or not. When you treat every thought as if it will become a reality, you will be careful of what you focus your mind's attention on. When you have a negative thought, you must learn to *transform it into a positive one*. For example, if you are having a bad day please take a deep breath and, say to yourself, "Today is an easy day" or "It is wonderful to be alive." To use positive affirmations effectively you must *consciously eliminate the negativity around you*.

Choose an area or aspect of your life you want to change and then decide what you want. Open your heart and say each affirmation out loud, allowing it to penetrate your consciousness. Write affirmations on index cards or sticky notes and keep them with you as a reminder to repeat them regularly throughout the day.

Keep the following in mind when working with affirmations:

- Use the present tense. Believe your vision is becoming a reality.
- Be positive; always use positive terms.
- Negative affirmations bring about the negativity you are trying to avoid simply by focusing your thoughts on it.
- *I am, I will, and I can* are statements of self belief.

II. *Everyday Affirmations*

AFFIRMATIONS FOR EVERY DAY

- I love myself.
- I am at peace with the Universe.
- I am special and loving.
- I am safe and always protected.
- I am surrounded with loving and caring people.
- I am accepting and loving of other people.
- I trust my inner voice to lead me on the right path.
- I do all I can every day to make a loving world for myself and those around me.
- I am always connected with God and the universe.
- I am strong.
- I am intelligent.
- I am beautiful.
- I am a good person.
- I am smart.
- I am creative.
- I am open to receive blessings.
- I am relaxed.
- I am energetic.
- I am full of joy.
- I am courageous.
- I am a problem solver.
- I am kind and patient.
- I can grow.
- I can heal.
- I can let go of fear.

- ☞ I can change.
- ☞ I can be positive.
- ☞ I can handle my own problems.
- ☞ I can be honest with my feelings.
- ☞ I can succeed.
- ☞ I like myself more and more each day.
- ☞ I will gain more emotional strength each day.
- ☞ I will control my anger today.
- ☞ I will grow stronger each day.
- ☞ I will praise my children today.
- ☞ I will face my fears courageously today.
- ☞ I will take care of "me" today.
- ☞ I will manage my time wisely today.
- ☞ I will handle my finances wisely today.
- ☞ I will take risks to grow today.
- ☞ I am a winner.
- ☞ I am the best friend I have.
- ☞ I have the ability to handle anything that comes my way.
- ☞ I deserve to love and be loved.
- ☞ I am a good example for others.
- ☞ I am responsible only for my own feelings.
- ☞ There are beautiful things happening in my life daily.
- ☞ I am a rich treasure ready to be found.
- ☞ To be loved I must give love.
- ☞ There are always opportunities in my life.
- ☞ My possibilities are endless.
- ☞ I can handle all the changes that come my way.
- ☞ There is nothing I can not handle.

III. *More Affirmations*

AFFIRMATIONS FOR POSITIVE CHANGE

- I am open to all possibilities before me and know only good can result from change.
- I respect myself as I am growing and changing for my best and highest good.
- I expect good in my life, and I embrace all the good in my life.
- Today I am grateful for all the good in my life.
- I trust Higher Guidance to lead me in the direction of where I need to be.
- I am open to receive all good.
- I embrace change and accept it as part of my positive growth.
- I have the ability to see the bigger picture in all situations placed before me.
- I have all the resources I need in my life to handle whatever happens in my life.
- Today I make loving choices for myself and accept good into my life.
- I am committed to my growth and prosperity today.
- I am rich in my ability to compromise and let others into my life.
- I am loving toward myself in every way.
- I release the fear that keeps me from growing.
- I am responsible for taking good care of myself.
- I open myself up to the abundance around me.
- I am living in the moment where life is truly exciting.

- Today I have enough time to take care of what I need to do.
- I am open to the opportunities placed before me.

AFFIRMATIONS FOR HEALTH

- I am in control of my health and well being.
- I love and respect myself.
- I am full of abundant energy.
- I am healthy in all aspects of my life.
- I am in control of my own body.
- I love and care for my body and it cares for me.
- I am at peace with myself.

AFFIRMATIONS FOR ABUNDANCE

- I am successful in all that I do.
- I am always productive.
- I have a lavish and dependable income.
- Everything I touch returns riches to me.
- I respect my abilities and always work to my full potential.
- I always have enough money for what I need.
- I am rewarded for all the good work I do.

AFFIRMATIONS FOR PEACE IN YOUR LIFE

- I am always at peace with myself.
- I am always in harmony with God and the universe.
- I am filled with God's love.

- I am at peace with all who are around me.
- I am free to be myself.
- I am a forgiving, loving, and caring person.
- I am responsible for my own spiritual growth.
- I am worthy of love.
- I am responsible for my own life and always maintain the power I need to be positive and happy.

DAILY AFFIRMATIONS

Write a different positive affirmation on 30 index cards. Pick one card a day for each day of the month. The card you select is your affirmation for the day. When you get to the last card, start again.

To extend this daily affirmation process, write thirty different daily affirmations for each month of the year. Keep the cards in an index card file box and use the collection throughout the year, adding new ones as you need them. This is a great gift to share with friends and family.

Chapter 10:

I: Find Inspiration in Others

Many people believe there is nothing they can do about their world and the people in it. However, if you do not like your world, you *can* change it by changing your thoughts, thus changing your consciousness.

My clients seek my help because they are lost in our world and don't know how to find their way home. They feel struck with the inability to be happy. I help them use The Keys to change their consciousness by teaching them how to alter their thoughts and feelings about their problems and the problem people in their lives. When you shift your perception, you will find problems progressively fade out of your life, and you begin to see goodness everywhere.

One of my clients, Judy, was single and in her mid forties when she first contacted me. Having made a lot of money practicing law when she was younger, she was now able to take "Easy Street" and relax a little bit. Although she was a very attractive professional, Judy had never been married. She had nothing but fear and dread inside her, and she had no interest in anything or anyone.

Judy's deceased mother had been an overbearing, abusive overeater. Now in her forties, Judy was an emotional wreck who, although she was a very successful lawyer, had no self worth. Like her mother she, too, was an overeater who felt she was undeserving of losing weight or attracting true happiness.

In our work together, Judy used creative visualization, prayer, and affirmations. She learned that if she wanted the world around her to change, she had to change her inner world. Realizing how important she was, she became aware that everything she felt had an effect not only on herself but on the people around her. Now Judy is happier and thinner than she ever thought she had the right to be, and she shares her gifts of insight with others.

Another client, Sarah, was in her mid 20s when she came to me. One day she realized, rather than attracting lots of friends and happiness, she was attracting conflict into her life. She lived paycheck to paycheck. Although she excelled in her career, she had trouble avoiding drama with her coworkers. The truth is Sarah worked very hard at her jobs to earn the favor of her managers.

You see, when Sarah, the youngest of four, was five years old, her parents became emotionally distant to the children when problems with the oldest daughter came to a head. They did the best they could as all parents do. If she cried, her father would ask her if she wanted something to cry about. He also would say regularly, "If I wanted your opinion, I'd ask for it." As a result, Sarah took care of herself emotionally and built a wall around her emotions to appear strong.

Sarah grew into what appeared to others as a very hard, strong, confident woman who rarely cried. She didn't tolerate others well. She had a handful of close friends she could rely upon, and she would do anything for them. Her friends were like her family. She married her high school sweetheart at the age of 21. He was a warm, funny, well-liked man who loved her unconditionally. His family accepted Sarah and showed her what it was like to love and support each other regardless of the challenges the family faced.

One day she realized she wasn't really happy with this person she had created. She wanted people to like her, not fear her. She wanted lots of friends. She wanted to be happy. One thing to know about Sarah is, when she set her mind to it, she could accomplish anything. Her mother always told her that you can be and do anything you desire as long as you're willing to work hard enough. Sarah always had a strong work ethic, and she had her whole life mapped out by the age of 18. But she wasn't happy.

People loved to complain to Sarah, and Sarah fed their negativity by agreeing with them. The truth is, she was afraid to disagree. She started to realize she was attracting this negativity to herself. She knew happiness had to start with positive thoughts. First, Sarah had to change her way of thinking to release the negative thoughts occupying her mind. It was not easy, but as I mentioned earlier, Sara was tenacious. Something very interesting happened. As she focused on seeing the good in everything, stopped feeding others' negativity, and became tolerant of others' differences, she started to attract kinder treatment from others and feel more positive about herself.

Sarah was raised Catholic. Her family, with the exception of her father, would attend Sunday mass every week and sit in the front pew. However, there was no religious presence at home. Religious education classes were something she had to do. She never embraced her faith; it was force-fed to her. When she was at the rehearsal for her confirmation, she decided this was not what she wanted and she walked away from it all. It always seemed to her it was more for show, not an inherent part of her life. She grew to avoid the G word. She wasn't sure she even believed in God.

Going through this transformation as an adult, Sarah found her faith. While reading a book about inner peace, she actually had to replace the word "God" in her mind with "Universal Power." You see, she knew there was some power greater than herself, but she wasn't yet ready to call it God. Every morning she would wake up and say, "I am grateful for the gifts I have received and for those I am about to receive." During the day she would take moments to nurture her faith through gratitude for all the blessings she was receiving.

Sarah held a vision in her mind of the person she was meant to be. This person was kind, tolerant, peaceful, and happy. She was surrounded by friends and supported by people who loved her. Financially, she was comfortable. Throughout the day and evening she would see this vision of herself as her current reality. She would recite these affirmations to herself:

- I am kind.
- I judge no one.
- I am calm and peaceful.
- I am happy. (She always said this with a smile.)

And she would pray. Over time, she became more comfortable with the word "God." Sarah would pray for help when she needed it, and she was never let down. She was surrounded by friends, strengthened her own relationship with her parents, let go of her need to control everything, and attracted a job which brought her financial security and amiable relationships with coworkers who respected her. She became the top salesperson in the company and a model of success and happiness in all areas of her life.

Using The Keys, Sarah let her heart open and became the person she was meant to be. And you can too.

The following are stories of some of my client's told in their words and printed with their permission. May their journeys inspire you!

II. M.M.

When Mary Ann spoke to our group of physical therapists about Reiki, energy work, and her experiences working with something she called The Keys to help her clients, I felt an immediate connection. At that time I didn't realize the extent of this connection or the journey that I was about to embark on.

What possessed me to call Mary Ann I thought was a mystery then, but now I understand it as the laws of attraction. I was desperately looking for answers and input as far as what direction I should go in reference to my life and the relationship I was in. Mary Ann seemed to have shown up at the right time in my life where I was seeking answers on how to change my life.

I had been seeing a counselor for help in dealing with a ten year relationship that was not working for me. I was desperately looking for direction on how to bring about positive changes in my life. Little did I know that a few sessions with Mary Ann were far more beneficial for my well being than the few months of sessions I had with the counselor. Mary Ann has an uncanny intuition and immediately helped me feel at ease. During our work together she introduced me to The 4 Keys. After a few sessions I was able to start releasing my feelings of negativity, I started to have the faith that I can change my situation for my best and highest good. I started to live a life of gratitude. I have been able to put out to the universe the visions of what I wanted out of my life and held those images in my mind. I learned the power of "prayer" and "affirmations".

In talking with Mary Ann and taking the time to implement The Keys into my life, things started to change and become clear. I felt like a huge weight had been lifted off of my back.

I had been in a counseling to help me deal with losing a relationship, but with the help of The Keys and Mary Ann's guidance I learned that I was not losing anything: the ending of my relationship was merely a stepping stone because I have learned that change is growth.

Today, I have evolved so much because of The Keys. I remember the first time I want to see Mary Ann, the doubts and negativity came in as I thought to myself that this session was going to be a waste of money, in that this person could not help me. These negative thoughts quickly disappeared because I learned that Mary Ann didn't *need* me to say anything. Somehow she just *knew* what I was thinking and what I was going through.

In the past I would struggle in new relationships with letting someone else "take care" of me, not in the literal sense, but, for example, by letting someone take me out for dinner, or letting someone surprise me with a weekend away. In my "past life" I was always the caretaker. Needless to say, even though I disagreed and thought that type of experience would be a welcomed change, she was right. It was very difficult for me to let these things happen, and when they did I laughed. Of course, my present partner thought I was a bit off the beaten path because every time she wanted to do something nice for me, it ended in a struggle, after which I would end up laughing, giving in, and fondly remembering what Maryann had said months before.

I had suffered from back pain for a long time. Doctors told me that there was nothing physical causing my back pain, so I brought it up with Mary Ann. She felt that my back pain was related to self inflected guilt. When I really thought about it, I felt horrible guilt about this ten year relationship that was ending. My thoughts were that I was a bad partner. There were feelings of guilt because I couldn't get rid of my partner's pain; I couldn't "fix" her. I had a constant feeling of walking on eggshells, living my life so as not to upset my partner. That is when I learned an invaluable lesson: I am not here to "fix" people; no one is. And that was not my job in the relationship. My job was to be a supportive, encouraging partner. My role should not have been the caretaker, and I really had nothing to feel guilty about. In trying to help, I learned that you can't help someone who doesn't want to be helped. Once I learned this lesson and released the guilt I felt, my back pain eased.

Over the past year I've referred many friends and patients to Mary Ann. This is something I normally would not do because there is always a worry that someone wouldn't be helped. True to her form, her track record in my small circle is unbelievable! There hasn't been one person I've referred to her who has been disappointed in her advice.

Maryann has been working on spreading the good news of The Keys for a number of years working with clients with complaints of physical pain as well as clients who are in emotional distress. It has been intriguing to hear about her work with various people.

Mary Ann and I were "thrown" together for a variety of reasons. Knowing Mary Ann has been a life-changing experience which enabled me to stop beating myself up and therefore start living my own life. I learned to not be afraid to follow my heart and my own intuition and that the universe will always take care of itself and me. Today I have evolved so much because of the use of The Keys in my life. My days of self doubt are a thing of the past.

III. L.G.

One day my doctor had discovered a nodule on my thyroid and how frightened I was. I am a nurse and in my mind I had constructed worrisome scenarios about the outcome. My first thought was to call Mary Ann, she has been a friend of mine for over 20 years, and I knew she would have some words of wisdom and encouragement

Mary Ann talked with me about her ideas of The Keys and suggested we get together to go over them. I did this gratefully. With her help, understanding and knowledge, I discovered how to visualize the positives, to really see and feel what I wanted; not just say" I want" and walk away waiting for it to happen, but to see the actual event in my mind. So I visualized that there was no node on my thyroid, and let it be. At my next check up the node was gone.

The Keys have taught me about trusting in the universe, that what we throw out to the universe returns to us, so if the thoughts are positive, they return to us in a positive manner, as well as if you send negative thoughts negative things come in return. The old adage "Be careful what you wish for" is so true! Maryann brought me out of my "closed" way of thinking and accepting life. She showed me that I can have what I want through positive thinking and by belief in a higher power, and she taught me to relax and let go of worry and anxiety.

IV. K.W.

When our teenage daughter underwent a "psychological crisis" we trusted Mary Ann to guide and counsel her back to a more positive place. Mary Ann taught our daughter about The Keys and how to apply them to her life. By using They Keys our daughter had learned that she has control over what happens in her life. She has learned that her thoughts are what makes things happen in her life. This can either bring about happiness or sadness, but this was her choice. This is not to say she still does not struggle with things in her life, bit know she has tools to use when she encounters a speed bump.

I have learned a lot about The Keys myself, and the beauty about them is that they are simple solutions to most problems. If you release the negativity, have faith and an attitude of gratitude; focus your mind to your true vision and use positive affirmations there is nothing you can't do in your life.

I am so happy that she has shared her gifts with others in her positive new book about a path toward a fulfilled life.

V. It Begins With You

- *Be in this moment.*
- *Be exactly who you want to be.*
- *Acknowledge you are great.*
- *Appreciate yourself and others.*
- *Keep a clean conscience.*
- *Honor the highest range of affection.*
- *Live in the belief of good will.*
- *Give of yourself when needed.*

It begins with you. What you fear you will draw to you. What you resist will persist in your life. What you think, you become. You want the world to change? Change your inner world and the rest will follow.

Epilogue:
Where Do I Go From Here?

The Keys are straightforward, highly effective tools you can use to live the life you where meant to.

Key 1: Release Toxic Emotions

Focus on the positive to eliminate the negative. When those surrounding you are emanating negativity, stay the course with your positive thoughts. Do not agree with them verbally as this will feed the negativity and draw you in. Saying nothing is the best response. "I can see how you would feel that way" is a great phrase to use if you feel the need to say something.

Key 2: Nurture Faith With Gratitude

Faith is the emotional attitude which says "yes" to life, and faith is like a muscle: the more you use it, the stronger it becomes and the more power you have to bring the virtue of your spirit into actuality. Remember, there is abundance for the person who will trust in the universe and go with the tide instead of trying to swim against it.

In order to nurture faith, you must have a relationship with God. There are 5 basic steps to have a relationship with God:

- *Know God*
- *Trust God*
- *Love God*
- *Embrace God*
- *Thank God*

Expect the best and live so that the best may become part of your experiences.

Key 3: Think And Create.

Remember your thoughts, attitudes, and feelings are the "parents" of your experiences. By ordering and disciplining your mind, you can consciously create circumstances, produce conditions, and control your destiny.

You have choices:

- *You can let your uncontrolled thoughts create the moment.*
- *You can allow your creative consciousness to create the moment, allowing a new idea from a higher source than your intellect can summon.*
- *You can allow the collective consciousness to create the moment, allowing your conscious and subconscious mind to bring something to reality.*

Your thoughts determine the world you see and the life you live: happy thoughts will create happy feelings and experiences;

negative ideas foster negative experiences. Through constructive thinking you can change the path of your life from negative to positive.

Key 4: Pray

Prayer is an invitation to welcome God into your life. Most people believe they must meditate in order to summon the power of prayer; in fact, every word that comes out of your mouth, every thought, every feeling is a prayer, and a prayer is always answered. When you speak, think, feel, and pray from your heart, mind, and spirit, it is communicated to God. Prayer is a conscious, intentional contact with the Supreme Power.

The power of prayer stands on your intentions. Focus on your prayer already being answered, not on the chance of it being ignored. Prayer is never about the words you speak; it is about the conviction with which you express the words, and without love, no matter how beautiful the prayer, it is empty and useless. Effective prayers are infused with love.

When you apply the four Keys to your life you become an adventurer. Use The Keys to align your body, mind and spirit. If your spirit is unlocked and opened, your life will be full of riches, both material and spiritual. Just as you are the only one who can put up road blocks and detours, you alone have the power to knock down these obstacles. You will enjoy every moment of your journey when you allow your creativity to run freely, your body, mind, and spirit attuned to the One Source.

What happens inside each one of us directly impacts our life experiences. Recognizing this compels us toward harmonious, purposeful living. You will overcome difficulties by applying spiritual disciplines to everyday life situations, because nothing can change or improve on the outside until you fix it on the inside first.

You will enjoy true abundance when you intentionally choose money, health, or love to enter your life. When you move about your life with clear intentions and are willing to cooperate with your innate wisdom, you will feel a deep sense of "at-one-ness", tranquility and peace. Use The Keys as a tool to help you release your inner creative power to generate goodness and abundance in your life.

No matter what religion we subscribe to, most have the same intrinsic goals. Notice the similarities between these "Golden Rules":

Brahmanism: This is the sum of duty: Do not unto others which would cause you pain if done to you.

Buddhism: Hurt not others in ways that you yourself would find hurtful.

Christianity: All things whatsoever you would that men should do to you, do even so to them.

Confucianism: Do unto others what you would have them do to you.

Islam: No one of you is a believer until he desires for his brother that which he desires for himself.

Judaism: What is hateful to you; do not to your fellow man.

Zoroastrianism: The nature alone is good which refrains from doing unto another whatsoever is not good for itself.

Taoism: Regard your neighbor's gain as your own gain, and your neighbor's loss as your own loss.

When you direct your life toward your higher self you yearn to connect with the One Source that creates and sustains all things, you unlock life's treasure chest. No longer driven by the motive for personal gratification, you will live for something much greater than yourself. This will lead to personal transformation and lasting fulfillment.

Your adventure in your new life will test as well as satisfy and complete you. Many times you may feel fearful as you face the unknown, and your mind will try to second guess your choices and talk you out of your resolve. Remember, due to past experiences your mind is limited, but with practice and perseverance, you can change your self-perception. Hold steadfast with courage and faith: by nurturing a relationship with God you will be able to heal all your own wounds; reconstruct your personality, and function as a balanced and enlightened person.

Let your days and nights be a reflection of the highest ideas from within your soul. Allow the "here and now" to be filled with the beautiful Light of God. Do whatever it takes to stay in touch and connected with God and your truth. Enjoy everything and need nothing.

This treasure chest of possibility is inside you. You are on a journey to realizing your true self and the person you were meant to be. Use The Keys to unlock the treasure chest; open the lid and dive in to the fortune of your life.

Author Bio

Mary Ann Dawson, PhD performs energy healings and leads prayer and Bible study groups focused on spiritual healing. She teaches clients how to transpose negative energy to positive energy, helping them to use their God-given talent to give back to the community and to make our world a better place.

In her personal quest for spiritual empowerment, she first learned about the human body's ability to heal itself and was blessed to study with Reiki Master Charles Ferraro. Next, she received a scholarship to participate in the University of Metaphysics and the International Metaphysical Ministry. In 1998 she was awarded a Bachelor of Metaphysics degree and in 2000 earned a Masters in Metaphysical Science. An ordained Metaphysical Minister, in 2002 Mary Ann completed a doctoral degree in Metaphysical Counseling. She continued her studies with the University of Sedona and became a workplace chaplain.

A spiritual advisor, healer, Reiki master teacher and practitioner, Mary Ann lives in Connecticut with her husband John, daughter Bianca, son Blake, 3 Akitas, and 8 cats.

Keynotes

Use The Keys to unlock yourself from the chains that bind you! Claim your right to live life to the fullest!

The Keys

Key 1: Release toxic emotions.

Key 2: Nurture faith with gratitude.

Key 3: Think and create.

Key 4: Pray

Selected Bibliography

Anonymous. *The Impersonal Life*. Marina Del Ray: DeVorss Publications, 1941.

Bletzer, June G. *The Donning International* Encyclopedia. Norfolk/ Virginia Beach: The Donning Company/ Publishers, 1986.

Conner, Tim. *The Ancient Scrolls*. Hollywood, FL: Fredrick Fell Publishers, Inc, 1942.

Curtis, Donald. *Your Thoughts Can Heal Your Life*. North Hollywood, CA: The Wilshire Book Company, 1961.

Holmes, Ernest Holmes. *The Anatomy of Healing: Prayer and Science of the Mind*. New York: Penguin Putnam Inc., 1938.

Holmes, Ernest Holmes. *A Dictionary of New Thought Terms*. Marina Del Ray: Devorss & Co., 1991.

Myss, Caroline. *Anatomy of the Spirit*. New York: Three Rivers Press, 1997.

Myss, Caroline. *Why People Don't Heal and How They Can*. New York: Three Rivers Press, 1998.

Ponder, Catherine. *The Dynamitic Laws of Prayer*. Marina Del Ray: Devorss & Co, 1968.

Roth, Ron. *The Healing Path of Prayer*. New York: Harmony Books, 1997.

Skain, Annalee. *The Temple of God*. Marina Del Ray: Devorss & Co, 1958.

Twyman, James F. *Portrait of a* Master. Tallahassee: Findhorn Press, 2000.

Walsh, Neal Donald. *Conversations with God, Book 1*. New York: G.P. Putnam's Son, 1996.

Walsh, Neal Donald. *Conversations with God, Book 2*. New York: G.P. Putnam's Son, 1997.

Walsh, Neal Donald. *Conversations with God, Book 3*. New York: G.P. Putnam's Son, 1998.

Walsh, Neal Donald. *Abundance and Right Livelihood*. Charlottesville, VA: Hampton Roads Publishing Company, 1998.

Wee, Joseph J. *Wisdom of the Mystic Masters*. West Nyack, NY: Parker Publishing Company Inc, 1968.

Printed in the United States
140403LV00003B/5/P

9 780595 483655